SO, Y
SALES...

*Challenges to fuel
your success
(and keep you sane)*

AMY RECZEK

Quantity sales: Discounts are available on quantity purchases. For details, contact us at the address below.

Sales and Presence – Amy Reczek
SalesAndPresence.com

Editor: Amy Collette
Cover Design: Melody Christian
Photo credits: Provided by pexels.com unless otherwise noted

So, You're in Sales.../Amy Reczek. 1st ed.
ISBN 978-0-578-62647-5

Disclaimer: Although every effort has been made to provide the best possible information in this book, neither the publisher nor author is responsible for damage incurred as a result of use or misuse of this information. This book is not a substitute for professional services.

BONUS

As a salesperson, you need all the tools you can get. This book is your first tool. For more free resources to help you reach the success you want, go to:

SalesAndPresence.com/bonus

Get instant access to exclusive bonus content, including irresistible email subject lines that will get you noticed.

PRAISE

If you haven't attended Amy's presentation *The Secret to Gaining Clients*, it's a must! She did an amazing job of sharing great techniques on how to gain clients. Amy's presence and confidence are infectious, and the knowledge she shares is so helpful and easy to implement into our daily business practices. I have already put her techniques to work. Thank you for educating me!—**Tonia Martinez**

I recently attended one of Amy's classes and was thoroughly impressed with the content and the audience she attracts. Within a day I landed my first meeting using her updated sales techniques by reaching out using social media and mirroring! I have landed more meetings with prospects using this technique than I ever would have just "cold calling." As I told Amy, "THIS REALLY WORKS!"—**R. Kristofer Claps**

Amy is one of the best things to happen to me professionally and personally. Her coaching, advice, and insight has helped me grow my business at every opportunity. I highly recommend Amy to anyone looking to refine their selling skills and master the art of pitching with your presence in addition to your words.
—**Andrew Dort**

I thought I knew it all before Amy's training. But her wisdom and insight is different from other coaches I've worked with. Amy's approach is to foster what we all want in business relationships—real authenticity and deep trust.
—**Amy Collette**

Amy Reczek's *Own the Room* event was terrific. I appreciated the nuts and bolts strategies she taught, and I gained takeaways that I could put into action immediately. I highly recommend this training to anyone looking to improve their sales, networking, and communication skills!
— **Sharon Heller**

GRATITUDE

It takes a village, and success does not come without the support of others. Thank you to all my clients, managers, team members, connections, and mentors I have learned from throughout the years and continue to learn from daily.

And to my husband, who encouraged me to write this book. It would not have happened without you. I am so grateful for you—your love, support, strength, and belief that I can do anything I set my mind to. You mean everything to me, inspire me daily, and are the best partner to do this thing called life with. I love you.

"Every champion was once a contender who refused to give up"

~ ROCKY BALBOA

CONTENTS

INTRODUCTION

Welcome, you awesome salesperson, you! You are awesome because you picked up a random book on challenges to better your craft.

You are also awesome because you are in sales, a career that is highly rewarding and hella challenging. You are on a high one second due to a great call, or finally closing that hard deal, getting face time with that person you never thought you would (holy crap, they actually answered the email!). Then, BAM! "How are your numbers looking for next month?" "Why didn't you get traction from that client yet?" "Nothing is updated in your CRM..."

As you know, sales is not for the faint of heart, or really anyone who wants to be liked most of the time. The word NO is constantly at the forefront.

You have rejection down to a science! It just rolls right off and you're on to the next call!

If only that were fully true. You do have tough skin though, and the longer you are in sales, the more tools you have to work through rejection more easily. However, you are human. So how nice is it that the crazy career you have chosen is shifting to a more human element?

During my time in direct sales, it was clear early on to me that all selling was—and is—communication. However, *how* that communication is delivered and nurtured is key. If I went barreling into a conference room and overloaded them with information on my services, which by the way, I was trained to do, it never would have worked. (I call this "throwing up on ourselves." We salespeople love to do that. We get excited. And then we kind of lose all sense of normal for a bit.) I bet you have tried it. I sure as hell have. How did it go? How did it feel? It sucked and felt like crap to me.

In business, we all need each other. One piece cannot run effectively without the others, so we choose who we are going to do business with to excel. Our clients choose which partners to put on the bus with them to make those wheels go round. Why shouldn't it be you? It should be. And you can show them why. But not with just your product and customer service.

I don't know about you, but I have taken more sales classes than I can count around product and how to pitch it. The problem with that is that now with technology, everyone already knows your product, which means they already know your pitch. So, what does that leave you with to get in the door as a salesperson? What's your differentiator? You have to know your product and pitch, but that does not get you in the door.

What does get you in? It is who you are and how you can help the client. It is how you are showing up. You have to show a bit of you. It is not enough to just work for a certain company. Authentically showing you creates the connection. When we are so caught up in the numbers and quotas, that truth can easily get lost.

My pivotal moment in realizing that the product I sold really didn't matter (due to it being a commodity) was a meeting I had about a year into my career. I was still totally green and 110% winging it. I got a meeting with a "Big Fish" client.

My presentation was perfect—all about the product and how it can "Help them and save money." "Our team has great customer service." "And we integrate with all systems." "Blah, blah, blah." I said everything right, everything I was taught in those oh-too-often sales meetings. Shocker that every other competitor who sold the same thing was *saying the same thing*. These C-level executives were wondering how the hell I got past the gatekeeper and actually landed this meeting, wonderfully wasting everyone's time.

The President of the company looked annoyed and bored. He finally looked at me and said, "So tell me why I would go through the upheaval of my entire system and have all of my employees relearn passwords and system integrations just to save fifty cents a transaction?"

In that split second I had a choice to keep "throwing up on myself" with all the product knowledge, or have a true conversation. He was absolutely correct, there was no reason for him to change all of that for a minimal cost savings. Except there was one major difference between the company he was currently using and the company I worked for.

I said, "Because you have me. I am employed by my company but I work for you. I work with your company goals to ensure the products you utilize with me meet and exceed those goals. I am a partner in your success, not another vendor."

What did I have to lose? The prospective client clearly wasn't impressed with anything during the meeting up to that point. He had challenged me to authentically show up. To start my journey of relationship sales. And at the time, neither one of us knew it.

That company ended up being my best and longest client. They moved with me through three different companies without question. They were willing to go through the upheaval of their systems each time. They paid more each time. Why? *Trust.* And partnership. Their goals were my goals. We were a team, not a vendor and a client.

You are the differentiator. You work for your clients.

You are my *Why* in creating these pages. I love the art of relationship selling and have a passion for teaching it. My challenge to you is this: during your time with this book, write down what jumps out at you, what you can use, the things that excite you—that challenge you. (Blank pages at the end of the book are available for you to take notes.) Then start putting them into practice.

This book is designed to take you from good to great. To challenge you outside of your norm. The goal is to create a different view from where you have been sitting. Because, let's face it, the same view gets old and stale. Let's freshen up what you do and create success along the way.

LET'S DANCE

---

*"Fall down seven times, get
up eight."*
~Japanese Proverb

It is not enough to just market your product or company. People have everything at their fingertips today. They already know (whether correct or not) the product you are selling—thank you, Google. They want to buy, not be sold. They want to feel connected. They want and need partnership. They know multiple companies and people they can buy the same product from. So why would they choose you?

Trust.

How? They need to feel they can relate to you. People do business with those they know, like, and trust.

Show yourself! Your cadence and branding demonstrate how you work. Building a relationship also gives you insight into who they are.

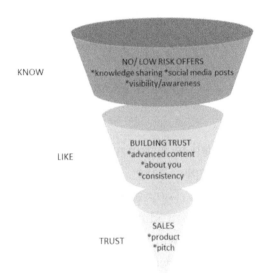

You know that feeling when you are killing it! Emails and calls get returned. Meetings are rocking. When everything is running on all cylinders, it feels like a dance between you and the (potential) client—it flows well.

And when it doesn't, it feels like you have two left feet. The rhythm somehow changed and you didn't get the message. It happens to every salesperson on the planet, and we all hate it. So how to get back into that dance? Make sure you are still being seen, get creative and change the dance.

Let's break it down...

Definitions

Sales Cadence

Sales cadence is simply a timeline of **sales activities and methods** that reps follow to engage leads.

The cadence is the *how* within your touchpoints. Whatever you are using to track your touchpoints, a customer relationship management (CRM) tool or Excel spreadsheets, your sales cadence lives within it. And here's the best part, no longer does your sales cadence have to be boring.

Personal Branding

Personal branding is the practice of **marketing people and their careers as brands**. It is an ongoing process of developing and maintaining a reputation and impression of an individual, group, or organization.

Your personal branding is *how* you are showing up in your cadence. This is giving the world *more of you*. Likeability. Relatability.

Personal Story: Being Seen

A few months ago, I was checking out at a clothing boutique near my house. I paid with a card, so my name came up. The lady (I now know she is the owner of the store) said, "Oh! You are Closing Deals In Heels!" (My Instagram handle). She recognized me by following me and felt like she knew who I was on some level. This is being seen. This is the *Know* part of know, like, and trust.

Client Story: Know, Like, Trust

I was invited to lunch with a potential client and my referral partner (who also was still working to get the client's business). This scenario doesn't happen all that much, but when it does, I attend. The only person I knew at the table was the referral partner. I did my research on the business and manager who was at the lunch. We made the typical small talk, learning about his business and what he needs. I then pointed out (due to his mentioning what he needs) that I have a networking event each month that might help with making his team more visible (the *Know* factor).

Later on in the meeting, I mentioned that I grew up singing. His daughter loves to sing! So many questions! It was a great conversation. (Here's the *Like* factor, due to a commonality). Before I had a chance to follow up with him, he friended me on Facebook (*Trust* factor). It was all about authentically learning about him, both professionally and personally, to find common ground and how I could help.

TAKE ACTION!

Your Challenges:

- ➢ Be seen
- ➢ Consistency
- ➢ Email
- ➢ Creativity

CHALLENGE: Be Seen

This is your general cadence. That *Know* area. Be decisive about the social media platforms you use and the networking events you attend. Start small, as this can easily become overwhelming. The intent is visual, so you are not out of view of your potential and current clients. Don't be out of sight and out of mind.

➢ Choose which social platforms you are comfortable with having a business page on. For example, LinkedIn, Instagram, and Facebook. How many times a week will you post?
   Note: If you want to keep it 100% business, opt for LinkedIn only as your social media platform.

➢ Decide on the email content you want to send. Will it be educational or industry related? Want to share events around town? Is this a monthly newsletter?

➢ Pick a number of networking events. How many networking events will you be going to each month? Three?

Five? Make sure to have a goal at each one. Find events you like, that have a good mix of people. Continue to go to those, instead of jumping around each month.

➢ Goal ideas for networking events: walk out with three new business cards, work on your personal intention while there, and ask a new rapport question. Rapport questions build trust. These go beyond "What is your name?" "What do you do?" A rapport question asks key information about that person.

Rapport Questions

Questions to build rapport:

> ➢ What are you excited about in the coming quarter (month, end of year, etc.)?

> ➢ What did you do over the weekend (holiday, summer, etc.)?

> ➢ What do you enjoy doing? (Notice this is not specific to work.)

> ➢ How can I be of help?

Make these yours, and work one into your qualifying questions (along with name, career, etc.). Word these questions in a way that is comfortable to you. Rapport questions build *trust*. And yet again — you stand out!

CHALLENGE: Consistency

We all know we need to be consistent. How easy do you find that to be? Unless you have a precise outline each week, it can easily be exhausting. Go here, post here, and respond there... like that.

If we focus solely on the *Know* part of the funnel, we will never move the potential client to forward action. We need to nurture the *Like* and *Trust* factors, too.

You have decided on the platforms—now decide how many posts per week, and what days. You decided on a monthly newsletter, now decide the day and time each month it will be sent.

If it helps, put these dates on your calendar. Example: Every Tuesday, Wednesday, and Friday by 9 am you are going to post to social media. The second Tuesday of the month you are going to email the newsletter.

Tips for you social media peeps:

➢ You can post on Instagram and link it to your business Facebook page so it will automatically also post there.

➢ Then copy and paste it to LinkedIn.

➢ You can prepare your posts for the week or the month so that you are not constantly focused on this. Views and open rates are higher mid-week.

CHALLENGE: Email

Email can be a total pain in the ass. Coming up with subject lines, *ugh*. What to say besides the old, "Seeing if you have time for a meeting..."

Email can come across as very stale. You might sound quite professional, but no one cares. Don't be unprofessional—obviously—but do be different.

Here are the four key components to a strong email:

1. Subject Line

➢ Keep it short (open rate goes up roughly 35% with short subject lines).

➢ Grab attention. You are looking for action or response from the person on the other end, right? You have to get them to open that email first!

Subject line ideas for you:

➢ **Have you tried <x>?** (The name of a new restaurant, show in town, place to hike, etc.)

➢ **If you're struggling with <x>, you're not alone!** Everyone in your industry struggles with common things—point them out and solve them in a new way.)

➤ **<Name>, you are busy!**
Do your research! Did they just win an award or do an amazing amount of business? Everyone reacts to seeing their name and being noticed.

(For more subject lines and other helpful resources, visit SalesAndPresence.com.)

2. Reference

Mention where you met them or the place you found them.

Examples:

I came across your information on LinkedIn...

It was nice to connect at the recent networking event at the new restaurant downtown...

3. Common Ground

If you met them somewhere and had a conversation, mention what they talked about. Note: What *they* talked about, not what you talked about.

Example: It was interesting to learn how you are utilizing specific marketing to increase your sales...

4. Don't play ping pong

Do you lob the meeting question over? Something like, "Would you have some time open in the coming weeks to set a meeting?" So many (bad) things are happening in this scenario:

- ➤ You just gave them a back door to say no.
- ➤ You don't look like the expert or in control.
- ➤ Your confidence is lacking.
- ➤ Time is wasted for both of you as you create the ping-pong effect of back-and-forth emails about nothing.

Instead, be direct. For example. "I would like to schedule a meeting to learn more about how you are creating success this quarter. Would Tuesday the 12th at 8:30am work for you? If so, I will send an invite your way."

You can also give an option of a few dates and times if you are more comfortable with that. This puts you in control, they respect you, and you get the meeting.

Two more pointers for this. Take out modifying words (just, maybe, hopefully, etc.). They lessen the tone of your email. And notice that nothing was pitched. Not your company, not your product, not you. Always make it about them.

For those of you who use an automated scheduler, be mindful about how it reads. You are wanting the meeting and they are doing the work... so make it inviting and easy. In your email with the link, state something like, "I know you are busy, so to cut down on back-and-forth emails, I have included the link below to my calendar for you to pick the best day/time that works for you". The calendar meeting names will default to things like "30 minute session," so also make this more inviting. For example, "Coffee or cocktails at your favorite spot in <area of your choice>." This does a few things. It lets them feel a part of what they are picking, and if you set up the area, then they focus on that as well and you don't have to worry about getting to your next meeting because it is too far away.

Email Example

Subject Line: <u>Wednesday, August 28th!</u>

Scott,

It was nice to meet you briefly at the <u>Networking Event last week</u>. Thank you for taking the time! I enjoyed our conversation around how you are <u>utilizing specific marketing to increase your sales</u>.

I would like to learn more about your business and the great things you are accomplishing. Are you open <u>Thursday the 12th at 9:30 am to grab coffee?</u> Please let me know if that works for you and I will send an invite.

Thank you, Scott, for your time. I look forward to connecting!

CHALLENGE: Get Creative!

Remember the dance? The potential client should be the one leading. That is when we feel the most rhythm; when they are feeling they are being heard, when problems are being solved for them, when connection is made because of something they talked about. We have two left feet when we push product and pitch. Take that out—that conversation will happen naturally. Instead, let's create.

Everyone has a preferred method to communicate, and we have quite a few ways to do this now. Mine is still email. However, that doesn't mean the person I am looking to connect with feels that way. Take notice of where your potential clients "live." Do they respond to email? Great! Phone? Okay! Neither? Are they always on Facebook? Send a note through Facebook Messenger. Same with LinkedIn. *Ask* about their preferred method of communication... What a concept! (Back to that direct, in-charge factor.) How awesome do you look now?

How else can you potentially open a door to conversation? How about sending a book on business or something that relates to what they do (please read it first!) Or send a text, a video message, repost something they posted that also speaks to you—and follow up with an email referencing it.

You have so many options. Keep your eyes open, and when you start to have two left feet—why not change the rhythm to get back into step?

PRESENCE

Finding your presence enhances every connection and communication you have, including your sales. It is the heart, the passion, the drive, the authenticity of you. We think communication—especially in sales—and we think words. We focus and train on our pitch, delivery, etc., yet there is another side of communication that is equally important to be aware of and to own. We communicate verbally *and* nonverbally. Your presence is your nonverbal communication speaking. It is how you carry yourself when you walk into a room, how you sit at a table, how you shake someone's hand... and so much more. This is your SUPERPOWER! And... you were born with it. We need to focus on our body language (nonverbal) communication as much as we do our verbal.

Think of the last time you were in a meeting, at an event, or anywhere that had a room of people, and one person in particular stood out. This person commands attention and seems larger somehow, takes up more space somehow. People are naturally attracted to this person.

This. Is. Presence. This is communicating without saying a word.

Up to 92% of how we naturally communicate is nonverbal. Are you using this advantage today? Probably not. Are you learning about your clients this way? Probably not. Are your competitors? No. And this is why you should be tapping into this. Plus, talk about killer communication skills! Hells to the yeah, you will be going from good to great in no time!

These are your "soft skills," your relationship selling skills, people!

Definition

Sales Presence

How: The ability to connect authentically and build relationships that inspire forward action.

Why: To build rapport and develop trust. This is each salesperson's key to developing trust.

In sharpening your presence, you differentiate yourself from competitors and make more of a positive impact with clients. Why do this? Because we are all human, and because most likely, what you are selling is a commodity.

Personal Story: History Lesson

I always loved the *how* factor in communicating, in analyzing a room. Having a psychology degree, I geek out on that stuff. Over the years in my career, it became clear that much more is going on during a meeting than what is verbally communicated. You can always tell who is annoyed to be there, who has the decision-making power, who the gatekeeper is, and so on, just by watching where they sit and how they interact with body language.

I wanted to take an actual class to understand nonverbal communication. When I started this company, I knew this was going to be a key element, but I also needed to have some credibility. Let's face it, this nonverbal stuff can seem fluffy to some. (You know who you are... hang with me, I promise it will be an aha moment for you.)

In came the Science of People. All they do is analyze and research nonverbal communication. And they had a training course to learn about it and then become a trainer in it. Yes! The application to get in was intense, and then the class itself was months long. There was so much more to this than I was thinking. Talk about aha moments going on all over the place! And... once you know it, you cannot unsee it. Just wait...

One of my aha moments was a lesson around how we actually communicate more nonverbally than verbally. In the training, I learned about the first Presidential debate ever televised. When you look at pictures or watch video, it seems Kennedy is much more confident. Obviously, we know who became president. But did you know this? Not everyone had a TV yet in their home. When they surveyed people who listened to the debate on the radio, they thought Nixon had won. The people who watched it on TV thought Kennedy won. Kennedy was prepped on body language, Nixon was not. There was not another televised presidential debate for 17 years because of this.

Nonverbal signals are 12-13 times more powerful than accompanying words.

Read that again.

And again...

It didn't matter if Nixon had a strong case in the debates on different topics, the nonverbal communication preceded the words.

Client Story: You Do That!

"Banks are big." I was thinking this as I walked into the building to present to a banking team. Banks are meant to feel that way—have you ever noticed that? They have presence just in the structure alone. Somehow, this always interests me and I find myself extremely aware of my presence when I am in a bank. Plus—I was presenting on relationship selling and presence that day, so my ass *better* be aware of it. During the presentation in this lovely, windowed board room, I was discussing the art of creating that space where you truly do own the room, where you connect on a level where people are drawn to you and want to engage with you. And that is when a woman in the meeting said, "You do that!"

Here's what she meant: Meetings start the moment you get out of the car. As I was walking into this larger-than-life building, I opened a door for random people (one who had too many things in her hand and almost spilled her coffee—we laughed and kept walking), and all got on the elevator together. A pretty normal morning. Usually, no one speaks on the elevator. But she did. She commented on my dress, asked if I worked in the building, and come to find out—she was attending my presentation. Did I mention that meetings start the moment you get out of the car?

In the middle of my talk about nonverbal communication and how to do that was when she got excited. "You do that! You did that this morning when holding the door and standing in the elevator. I felt like I needed to talk to you, to inquire about who you were! I can use this!"

Yes she can, and so can you. You carry yourself and communicate on a much larger scale than you realize. I walked into that building with intention. I was highly aware of what I was communicating without verbally saying anything. She noticed. They noticed.

The presence of bank buildings are designed to get noticed.

Use your presence. Get noticed. Start the connection.

TAKE ACTION!

Your Challenges:

> ➤ First Impression

> ➤ Trust Factors

> ➤ Mirroring

> ➤ Body Language

CHALLENGE: First Impression

We have all heard about making a good first impression. However, when was the last time you focused on your first impression when you walked into a room?

My bet is you are usually in your head and thinking of what you are going to say. This is your challenge: Instead of words, be mindful of how you are walking into a room. It is easier and harder than you think. Easy, because you innately have this ability. You are born with it. Hard, because we are ingrained to focus on our verbal approach, which we are constantly focusing on.

Frank Bernieri, Professor of Social Psychology at Oregon State University, conducted a study around the importance of first impression within a job interview. Applicants were interviewed for roughly 20 minutes. He then had observers watch only 20 seconds of the interview— focusing on the interviewee walking in. Both the interviewer and observers rated interviewees the same in warmth, competence and confidence.

You have 20 seconds to make a first impression, and it is not about what you say.

Two things you can do to make a powerful first impression:

Intention

Before you walk into any meeting, reset your intention. Yes, your end goal is to gain a client. But that is not your intention for this moment. This is a step to your end goal.

What are your steps for today? Say out loud or write down three intentions for this meeting today. Have them? Good. Is one of them to tell them your pitch or your product? Nope. Get rid of that and put something about *them* in its place. (This is totally odd when you first do it, I know—but do it and thank me later. It's like adding raisins into a pasta dish... I swear. You never knew you needed it.) Be specific and own it.

Possible intentions:

➤ Gain knowledge on potential clients' quarterly outlook.

➤ Notice your posture, how you are showing up without speaking. (What do you need to work on here?)

➢ Focus on right now. Your mind chatter is saying, "OMG, what a crazy day!" Take a moment to walk through your day, then put all of it aside. Refocus on the meeting. Visualize the players in the room, remind yourself what you know about them and the company. Re-center to the moment in front of you.

➢ Now, your attitude. Check it. It might sound odd, but your attitude and intention shine through when you walk in the door. This type of attitude is gratitude. While getting out of the car and walking to the building, say to yourself three things you are grateful for. This doesn't have to be focused on work. For example: the sun is out, I have loved ones, I get to do this... A couple things happen when you intentionally focus on gratitude:

1) The anxiety, nervousness, etc. lessens and is kept in check. Fun fact: Fear and gratitude don't live in the same space well together.

2) When focusing on gratitude, it also lets *you* shine through. It opens you up to invite response and engagement. Remember the elevator lady? Your *presence* is communicating.

➤ Think about the last meeting you just had. When you got out of your car you took what with you? Phone, padfolio, laptop bag, purse (ladies), maybe coffee or something for the group... Do you have the visual? What all was in your hands? If possible, do not hold anything in your hands while starting the meeting (remember, the meeting starts the moment you get out of the car). If you are carrying items in, either arrive early to do so or keep your arms open while carrying. For example, walking in with a padfolio in hand... hold it down and to your side, not across your body or with two hands (this is blocking—we want to stay away from that). Phone? *Put it away!* Head up, shoulders back and down. Invite that conversation in.

CHALLENGE: Trust Factors

What do you think we notice first in others? Eyes? Hair? Clothes? Smile? Height? Our trust factors are built in, and it goes back to caveman days when we watched other humans approaching to see if they would be a friend or foe. A foe would be carrying a club or some sort of weapon to take land or food.

Hands

Our trust factors are our *hands*. Most of us feel awkward about knowing what to do with them if they are not in our pockets (men, you are great at this), arms crossed, in our laps at a table....

Show them off!

If you take *one* thing from these pages it needs to be this:

We as humans are hardwired to subconsciously be aware of others' hands. In a split second we decide initially if we trust another person or not. How much easier would your life be if you used this up front to ease your potential client and start creating that trust before you ever spoke? Ways to keep your hands in view:

➢ **No pockets!** No arms crossed! Like, ever. Keep them by your sides and visible.

➢ **On the table.** When at a table, have them up on the table. This is one I am constantly working on. To get used to this, use stabilizers—hold something that makes you feel more comfortable, like a pen or a coffee cup.

➤ **Handshake.** We know to shake hands, but make sure you are intentional. No "dead fish" or "top handed" (horizontal handshake so that your hand is on top of theirs. This is a superior move).

Make your handshake medium firm, vertical, and with purpose.

➤ **Before the meeting.** Remember—the meeting starts before you ever walk into the room. Hands out!

CHALLENGE: Mirroring

Think about a friend you are very close to. Think about how you both act when you are together. You start to pick up the same mannerisms as the other, the same tone or inflections on words.

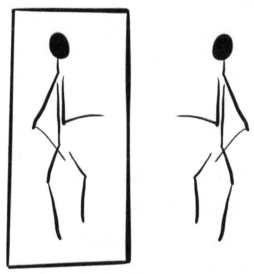

Image courtesy of Laura Pena Painting

A fancy word for this (that I can never pronounce correctly) is *chameleonization*. We do this both verbally and nonverbally. This is natural rapport building.

I was walking through the park after a run recently. A gentleman walked by, turned around and asked, "How do you like those headphones?" They are the new AfterShokz Trekz Air, if you care to know, and they are awesome. After a brief conversation about the headphones, he said, "Thank you, cheers!" and I said back, "Cheers!" I don't ever say cheers. That is a classic case of mirroring.

You do it all the time—now you just need to notice and refine it. Why? Rapport building leads to, yep you got it, *trust*! And trust leads to business and partnerships. You superstar, you!

Here are some ways to be aware and work on this (non-creepy-like), and remember—the key here is to be natural and authentic.

Mirror their email sign-off

Starting with the easiest, mirror their email sign-off. Whatever theirs is: Sincerely, Thank You, Best, Yours, change yours to it. This is extremely subtle and easy to do.

Mirror the platform they prefer

People communicate all over the place today, not just by email and phone. If they message you through Facebook

Messenger, stay there until they move out of it. Texting—that too. Note: if you are not getting any responses from a prospect, try one of these other ways to reach out. Your prospect might prefer it and it can get their attention.

Staying on your prospect's preferred platform (Facebook, texting, etc.) can be a bit more casual than a formal email. If they use emojis, send one back!

Body language

Be careful with this one, as it has the potential to come off wrong if it's too obvious. Work on this skill with those you know first. A few you can master:

> ➢ If they tend to hold a pen or a cup during a meeting, you do the same.
>
> ➢ Are they leaning? Lean slightly forward if they are.
>
> ➢ Arm rested on the back of the chair? You can do this also. Be aware of your audience on this one. It is a less "business" look and might come off unprofessional to some. It's all in the way you do it.

Those are some ideas to get you going. The biggest thing to remember with this and why you are doing it:

People like those who are like them.

Human nature to its core.

CHALLENGE: Take Notice

We all react to our environment. This means both you and your client. Notice how you act when you get a bit nervous at a meeting or presentation. Do you rub your arm, crack your knuckles, wring your hands, or bite your lip? All of these are examples of self soothing. We do this to calm our nerves.

Self soothing behaviors

Notice if you do some self-soothing behavior. (We all do it... welcome to the club.) What is your go to? First just take note of what you do and when you do it.

I self-soothe when I am sitting in a seat, on a plane, that is somehow balancing in the air. I travel a lot and love it. However, my mind cannot get the concept of a plane in the air. My body protects itself and calms my natural (nervous) reaction. I end up biting my lip. It is a comfort.

Once you have noticed how you self-soothe, work on adjusting it. Take baby steps here and remember your nervous reactions are comfort gestures. So also notice what you are reacting to. Can those nerves be moved into the excitement category?

How about your clients—are they doing these gestures? If so, a conversation will help. Some questions to consider:

➢ How are you sitting with what we have talked about?

➢ What do you feel would make this fit your needs more?

➢ How can we help and support you through this?

Negative body language

Another one to take note of is negative body language. What this looks like is arms blocked, eye avoidance, opening your laptop or phone and focusing on it.

If your client is doing this, I challenge you to question if it is the person or whether something is not a good fit for them (the day or time, the product, or you.) Maybe they are having a really crappy day and it has nothing to do with you. No reaction on your part is needed except to notice it.

If this is how they behave each time you meet or speak, possibly it's time to back off or move on. Not everyone or every company is a good fit.

To work on opening up a person, always have something to hand them. Don't give out your business card until you feel you need to or at the end of the meeting. Have a product slick or presentation folder? Give that to them so they have to physically uncross their arms. This is amazing to watch, as the negative moves out and they are open to the moment. Maybe they are not "all in," but a door cracked is an opening, right?

CHALLENGE: Head Nod

What? Head nod? Yes. Why?

To continue to learn about the people in front of you. To keep them engaged and talking. Remember that "pitch and product" is the last thing in your sales funnel. Don't get caught up in that. We need to practice shutting our mouths. The client should be doing most of the talking. I don't know about you, but this was one of the absolute hardest things for me... until I started doing it.

We know the saying, "You have two ears and one mouth, you should be listening twice as much as you are speaking." I like to visualize this in time. Normally you have an hour with a client, so use the 80/20 rule here. They should be speaking roughly 40 minutes, and you 20 minutes of the meeting.

How to keep your client talking and engaged:

Triple head nod

> Most of us do this to some degree already. Tilting the head slightly and nodding the head three times in a row at a medium

pace signals the person to keep talking. You are engaged in what they are saying.

Lean in. You can add this to the head nod but if you are just not feeling the whole head nod thing, lean in. A simple gesture that goes miles in saying, "I hear you! I'm interested!"

Tell me more

Another simple action to keep the focus on them. Simply say, "Tell me more." I learned this from a friend, entrepreneur, salesperson, and true badass. I was talking about something in general and she said, "Interesting, tell me more!" And what did I do? I got below the surface and told her more.

Everyone wants to be heard. We have all been in a setting where we felt like we were not being listened to, that they were just waiting to speak again.

Don't be that human. Listen and build the connection.

Feeling, energy, and influence matters.

Presence and cadence communicate with one another. If you are off on your presence you are forcing your cadence. Remember, you are the one communicating. Your well-planned cadence only works when you show up authentically. Don't be afraid to change things up to get back into that rhythm that feels good.

CHANGE IT UP

"Change is inevitable—
except from a vending
machine."
~ Robert C Gallagher

Let's get you unstuck, shall we?

We all get stuck.

Why?

Because we are creatures of habit.

If it works once, or five times, we think it will always work. Except the client changes and at some point what we think we are so amazing at doing... doesn't work. And here is the beauty in that—it shouldn't always work. First of all, how completely boring that would be, but most importantly—then you stop growing, learning, seeing, getting excited, and being challenged. All things that keep you on that road of getting to great.

We need to get stuck to be able to challenge ourselves and spice things up a bit. What do you have to lose?

Personal Story: Writing This Book

Write a book of sales challenges? Yep! I can do that. Totally easy. I have everything all over the place, written down, on the computer, and in my head.

I sat down to start. I got up and left it. Came back to start. Got up again. I was stuck! Why the hell is this so hard?! I talk about all of this daily!

Why? Because the format was out of my habit, my norm. I like to talk, not write. I had an original layout in my head of how this was going to go. What I thought was going to be the beginning of the book is now the ending. And instead of starting at the beginning, I started here. I had to challenge myself to change up what wasn't working. And voilà! I began to get unstuck.

Client Story: Changing His Style

This story is one of my favorites. I was teaching a class on gaining clients, and had all industries in the room. We were on a section about the importance of connecting within social media. Everyone does this a bit differently, however, one gentleman, originally from New York (I love you East Coasters—you know how you are) was adamant about not utilizing social media for business. There was great discussion around this and at the end of the class his stance remained. The next day, I got a message from him on Facebook. The day after that, another one asking to meet. We met at a networking event a few days later. He ran (OK, walked briskly, he was excited) from across the room to tell me what he had been dying to share. He showed me his correspondence with a potential client that he had been getting no responses from using email and calls. He messaged the client within Facebook. The potential client responded. He stayed within the platform the client was comfortable with (remember mirroring?). He got the meeting. This is his testimonial;

"I took Amy's advice and within a day I landed my first meeting using her updated sales techniques by reaching out using social media and mirroring! I have landed more meetings with prospects using this technique than I ever would have just cold calling. As I told Amy over coffee yesterday, 'THIS REALLY WORKS!'"

He challenged himself to do something new. He changed it up. He got unstuck.

TAKE ACTION!

Your Challenges:

- ➢ Change of Scenery
- ➢ Celebrate Others
- ➢ Create, Network
- ➢ Ask
- ➢ Refresh Button
- ➢ Research It

CHALLENGE: Change of Scenery

Change of scenery sounds so simple, but we always forget about it. It works.

I'm not talking about taking a time-out, although those are great for your mental health when needed. I'm talking about looking at things differently, literally. Here are a few ways to change it up:

Change your seat

Trust me. Move your chair to a different position at the desk. Maybe at the side of the desk, or across from where you are "supposed" to be. If you work remotely, you know your comfort places. Change it up for a week. Don't sit in the same spot you normally do. Go to new coffee shops, coworking spaces, etc.

Rearrange your desk

Move everything to opposite sides, and declutter while you are at it.

Stand Up!

If standing feels awkward while on your computer, stand up when you are on the phone.

Notice what is different around you. Start with one day. Can you do two? A week?

You totally got this.

CHALLENGE: Celebrate Others

We salespeople are notorious for getting in our own way. I totally get it. You have quotas, bosses, goals, and a life to pay for. It is easy to jump on that hamster wheel of worry. I have yet to find someone who enjoys that wheel or who has it work for them. You? Jump off of it (and start getting traction again) by shifting focus on to your potential and current clients—and away from you.

Kudos

When was the last time you sent a potential or current client kudos? Are you following them on Facebook and LinkedIn? You should be! Notice what those individuals are doing, as humans and as a company. Did they go on a trip, participate in an event, share a great quote, give back to the community?

Congratulate them

Like and comment on something they are doing that speaks to you. Send a quick email with the subject line: "Trip looked amazing!" "Congrats!" "So excited to see this!" And briefly comment on it. Notice that nothing was said about work or selling.

Keep it professional

Want to keep it more focused on business? Great! Do the same thing, but on a business level. When the company or person wins an award, their company is growing, they give back as a team, etc., send similar kudos with a brief comment. Again, nothing was said about work or selling!

A great app for sending kudos is Thnks. For the first meeting I ever have with someone I send them a "Thnks a Latte" text with a link to a free Starbucks coffee. You can send a group lunch or donate to a nonprofit in their name. The best part is: *You. Get. Noticed.*

CHALLENGE: Create

What does create mean to you? What feeling comes up when you read the word? Are you creative by nature (an artist, musician, etc.)? Do you think you don't have a creative bone in your body? Either is perfect.

Start with an interest.

A few months ago I went with a friend to an adult coloring book party. Odd? Yep. Fun? Totally. Did I have to be creative? Nope. Was I able to see things differently and with more clarity due to tapping into that creative side? Absolutely.

There is no wrong or right way to create. But please do create. It is your growth element!

Say hello to that creative badass side of yourself

Do you have a creative side? Do that! Turn the music on full blast and sing. Like words? Start writing. Like to paint? Pick up that brush. Whatever it is, tap into it. If you have no idea where to begin, order a coloring book on Amazon.

Creativity inspires us. Listen to a new sales podcast (or any motivational one), read a new book, or learn something new about your industry or your profession. When was the last time you invested in personal growth? Now would be a good time...

Creativity helps you see things differently and better deal with uncertainty."
~Courtney Carver

CHALLENGE: Network

Dare we say the word? Networking, connecting, whatever lingo you prefer, is an absolute must. Connecting and building your network maximizes your success. Most of the people you will meet probably won't be clients, but they may be referral sources. People love being helpful. When someone they know is looking for help with what you do, your network will tell them about you. But, they first have to know you are out there.

Events

You can find a networking event every second of the day. The challenge is to pick what is right for you. This might take a bit of work on your end. Look in Meetup or Eventbrite for business networking near you. Read through the descriptions. Contact the organizer and ask what you need to know: How often do you hold these meetings? (The more regularity, the better). What is your average attendance? Any specific industries you target?

Then look through the attendee list—who do you want to meet?

What is your purpose and goal? Maybe it is to meet and find out more about three new people. What about practicing your introduction or rapport questions?

Networking makes you visible. It is also a safe space to practice your skills. When was the last time you asked someone something different? Try it on! See how it feels! Is it uncomfortable? Yay! You are so on the right track.

CHALLENGE: Ask!

Ask anyone and everyone. Ask anything. Ask how they are creating. Ask how they are connecting with clients. Ask how they overcame not gaining a client. Ask what they see as your strengths. Ask. Keep asking.

Who else can you ask? *Your favorite client!* Have you ever done this? Everyone needs an ego boost now and again. And you can use their feedback to gain insight to use going forward. Hell yeah, they love you, you have worked hard to gain and keep them as a partner! Plus, your strengths shine through with your best client.

Maybe they will surprise you and point out something you didn't realize was coming through. Listen to what they respond with. I bet you it will be a mix of things you were and were not aware of. Perfect reason to do this! We do not fully understand how others see us until we ask. Once we know, we can be aware of incorporating these things into other client relationships.

Then, start asking them yearly how you're doing.

How to ask? "Hello my favorite client, I would like to schedule a time for a face-to-face review of my service to you." Point out at the meeting that this will be an annual tradition.

Review question ideas: (maybe start off with a few softball questions before you come in with the fastball):

> How has overall service been?
> Has anything changed that needs to be addressed?
> How do you feel my level of communication is with you and the team?
> Are items addressed in an efficient manner when they come up?
> What specifically am I doing for you that makes you keep choosing to do business with me?
> How can I help further?

Recommendation: Do this outside of the office or usual environment. You will have fewer distractions and more direct conversation. Go grab a coffee or a happy hour drink.

CHALLENGE: Refresh Button

You sell products and services primarily to an existing marketplace, and you are not the only one who does. That's good and bad news. Bad in that your product and services are a commodity, and everyone is doing similar things. Good in that you can learn from what others are doing, and that you are the differentiating factor.

The longer we are in an industry, the more likely we are to become stuck in a stale sales cycle. Let's hit refresh—liven it up a bit. Here are a handful of ways to do this:

Reset the numbers on the clock

You have a number to hit by a certain date. Start from now. Take it in baby bites. For example, you have a target to hit by the end of the month. It is the 10th of the month and you are behind in your goal. Instead of looking at the end number, break it up. Target a few lower-priced sales to equal the end goal. Do you have a current client you can upsell a new or adjusted product to? What about an intro client, who is on the fence and willing to start smaller? With these smaller goals, you work toward the end goal.

What about your content?

When was the last time you refreshed how you are communicating?

Content refresh ideas:

> ➢ Automated or canned emails? Change it up.
> ➢ Same presentation from five years ago? Yeah, it's time to update, don't you think?
> ➢ Send a video via text. What? It's totally nerve-wracking if you're new to it. But it works.
> ➢ Voicemail. Change it. Stand up and smile while you're recording!
> ➢ Make it random. Send a "Happy National _____ Day!" (nationaldaycalendar.com)
> Just the other day, a salesperson posted a 30-second video to Facebook of

himself eating ice cream and dancing to a song on the radio for National Ice Cream day. He got a ton of views and engagement.

➤ Are you always using phone and email? What about LinkedIn, Facebook, and Instagram messenger? If you are using a promotional marketing sales email, the open rate is only around 24 percent. Your audience is on multiple platforms these days, so you need to be also. Meet your clients where *they* are, not where you are.

Your end goal is *always* successful when you *focus on process*.

CHALLENGE: Research It

Research your clients. Your competitors. You.

When was the last time you googled a current client? Or yourself? (That might be scary, depending...) But really! We get complacent and think we already know everything we need to about all the above, including our own industry and services. Well, that just isn't true. Pull up your own website or your company website and look through it. I will bet you see something you forgot about!

Time block to research

> Make a list of who you are focusing on. Review and clean up your account list. (Who have you not reached out to each quarter? Who needs more attention?)

Alerts are your best friend

> They do the work for you. Of course, always do a bit of research to make sure what is coming through is accurate before touching base with a prospect, but these truly save you so much time. Some to consider:

➤ **Google Alerts.** An easy way to stay informed.

➤ **Talkwalker.com Alerts.** This service is free and a good alternative or addition to Google Alerts.

➤ **Mention.com.** There is a fee attached to this one, however it is a fairly robust service. If you work with a company, inquire about them taking on the fee.

NOTE: Remember to sign up for alerts from competitors as well, so you stay in the know! Use the information that's out there in your correspondence. It is about them and about trust, not about you!

Have a few prospects who *love* your competitor?

Figure out why. If it is a trust relationship and they will never move, then move on. Don't waste your time. If it is something else, that door will be cracked at some point, so stay in front of them with value-added information.

Choose three people and three companies you have never talked to.

Set the intention to get in front of them. Make sure you have a timeframe on that goal. Research. Meet them where they are. You know what to do, you rock star. In that timeframe did it work? It will. Stay centered in that intention.

EPILOGUE

Dance with your clients, check in with your presence, and change things up always.

Sales can be a rewarding, challenging, and exciting career. Continue to give yourself grace, learn and grow from others, all while enjoying the success you create.

Thank you for spending some time with me as you challenge yourself on your journey. I would love to hear about your challenges and successes! Reach me at:

SalesAndPresence.com

To Your Success,

Amy

ABOUT THE AUTHOR

Image by Merne Judson, III mernejudsonthethird.com

Amy is a Corporate Sales Coach and Professional Image Consultant, Speaker, Trainer, and owner of Sales and Presence, Inc.

She is dedicated to helping sales professionals, entrepreneurs, and companies increase productivity, lead with presence, and up-level relationship selling and communication skills. As a respected, high-level Senior Sales Executive with a distinguished 17-year career in the mortgage industry, Amy brings a wealth of practical knowledge, insight, strategies and support to clients.

Amy holds her Bachelor's Degree in Psychology from Concordia College, and has had extensive sales training, along with training on nonverbal communication at the Science of People. She combines this background to bring a unique and refreshing insight to the art of relationship selling.

She is an accomplished speaker and trainer on relationship sales- and presence-specific topics. During her sales career, Amy witnessed firsthand how bringing presence into the equation of communicating can improve not only the ability to close in a sale, but also improve communication across all company lines from CEO to HR.

Amy teaches her own classes, leads a monthly women's mastermind, and runs a successful monthly business networking event. Along with consulting, Amy makes time to be involved with community and professional organizations. She follows CMLA, DMAR, and MBA, is a founding member of RISE Collaborative Workspace, serves on the board of the Pediatric congenital heart association, has been featured in VoyageDenver Magazine, and is a member of the National Speakers Association.

Amy has called Colorado home for 18 years and lives in downtown Denver. She has a passion for travel, working out, cooking vegan food, experiencing live music, and experiencing anything new.

Connect with Amy at:
SalesAndPresence.com

NOTES

NOTES

NOTES

NOTES

NOTES

NOTES

NOTES

NOTES

NOTES

NOTES

NOTES

Made in the USA
Monee, IL
07 October 2020

44227524R10056